Th... the APOSTLE

....

Builder and Believer

First Century
Born in Galilee
Feast Day: July 3
Community Role:
Construction Worker and Architect

Text by Barbara Yoffie
Illustrated by Jeff Albrecht

Liguori

ONE LIGUORI DRIVE
LIGUORI MO 63057-9999

Dedication

To my family:
my parents Jim and Peg,
my husband Bill,
our son Sam and daughter-in-law Erin,
and our precious grandchildren
Ben, Lucas, and Andrew

To all the children I have had the privilege of
teaching throughout the years.

Imprimi Potest:
Stephen T. Rehrauer, CSsR, Provincial
Denver Province, the Redemptorists

Published by Liguori Publications
Liguori, Missouri 63057

To order, visit Liguori.org or call 800-325-9521.

p ISBN 978-0-7648-2557-6
e ISBN 978-0-7648-7008-8

Liguori Publications, a nonprofit corporation, is an apostolate of the
Redemptorists. To learn more about the Redemptorists, visit Redemptorists.com.

Printed in the United States of America
19 18 17 16 15 / 5 4 3 2 1
First Edition

Dear Parents and Teachers:

Saints and Me! is a series of children's books about saints, with six books in each set. The first set, *Saints of North America,* honors holy men and women who blessed and served the land we call home. The second set, *Saints of Christmas*, includes heavenly heroes who inspire us through Advent and Christmas and teach us to love the Infant Jesus. The third set, *Saints for Families*, introduces saints who modeled God's love within and for the domestic Church.

Saints for Communities explores six individuals from different times and places who served Jesus through their various roles and professions. Saint John Baptist de la Salle taught children and founded a familiar educational system. Saint Joan of Arc helped to bring peace to the country of France. The Apostle Matthew was a tax collector before deciding to follow Jesus. The Apostle Thomas preached and built churches. Saint Cecilia sang hymns to Jesus in her heart. And Michael the Archangel is well-known for his protection.

Which saint doubted Jesus' resurrection? Which one fought a heavenly battle? Which saint heard heavenly voices? Who sold everything he owned? Which saint was first named Levi? Which saint was married against her will? Find out in the *Saints for Communities* set—part of the *Saints and Me!* series—and help your child connect to the lives of the saints.

Introduce your children or students to the *Saints and Me!* series as they:

—**READ** about the lives of the saints and are inspired by their stories.

—**PRAY** to the saints for their intercession.

—**CELEBRATE** the saints and relate them to their lives.

saints of communities

 John Baptist
Teacher

 Joan of Arc
Soldier

 Matthew
Banker

 Thomas
Construction worker

 Cecilia
Musician

 Michael
Police officer

Jesus traveled from town to town and taught people about God's love. He healed the sick and helped the poor. Many people followed Jesus. They were called his disciples. Jesus chose twelve special men, called apostles, to preach his Good News to all nations. This is a story about the Apostle Thomas, sometimes called "Doubting Thomas."

The apostles were Jesus' close friends. They listened to him teach and tried to be good and kind. Jesus said and did amazing things. He healed the sick and fed the hungry. He even performed miracles, like walking on water and calming a storm!

One day, Jesus said, "I want to go see my friend Lazarus. He is very sick." The apostles were worried. Lazarus lived in the town of Bethany, near Jerusalem. People who did not like Jesus lived there, and someone might try to hurt him.

Thomas looked at the others and said, "Let us go with Jesus. We can die with him!" That was a very brave thing to say.

When they arrived in Bethany, Lazarus had already died. Jesus went to the tomb. He held up his hand and said, "Lazarus, come out!" Lazarus walked out of the tomb. Everyone was surprised—Jesus had brought their friend back to life!

Jesus taught the apostles about God the Father. Little by little they began to understand. One night, they shared a special meal. Jesus talked about many things. "I am going someplace very soon," he said. Thomas asked, "Where are you going? How do we get there?" Jesus answered, "I am the way, the truth, and the life."

Later they followed Jesus to a nearby garden. It was quiet there. They could pray together. Suddenly, soldiers came and took Jesus away. He was arrested, beaten, and put to death on a cross. His body was placed in a tomb. The apostles felt afraid and alone.

Three days later, Jesus came out of the tomb. He had risen from the dead! Jesus went to see his friends, but Thomas was not with them. "Peace," Jesus said. "Jesus, you are alive! Is it really you?" they cried. They were filled with joy.

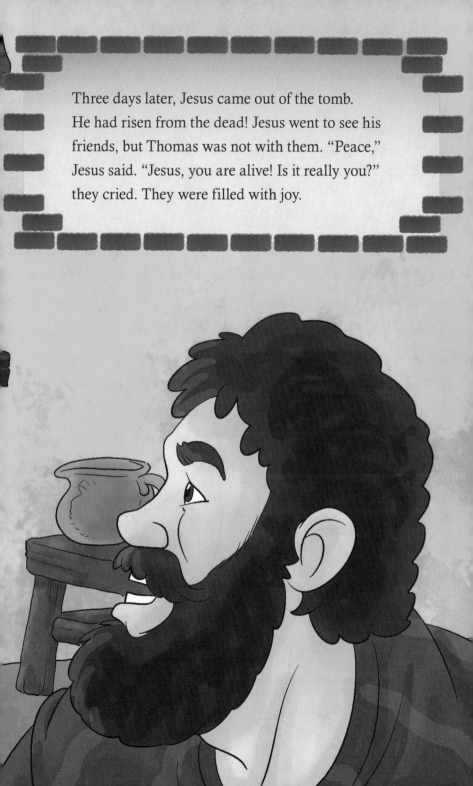

Some of the apostles ran to find Thomas. "Thomas, Thomas," they shouted, "Jesus is alive! We saw him!" "What do you mean? I do not believe you. I want to see the marks on his hands and his feet," Thomas told them.

A week later, the apostles were praying together, and Jesus appeared again. "Peace," he said. Thomas stood and rubbed his eyes. He looked at Jesus. Seeing the marks on his hands and feet, Thomas said, "My Lord and my God!" "Yes, Thomas, I am alive. Now you can believe," said Jesus.

Thomas did believe, and his faith grew very strong. One day, Jesus sent the Holy Spirit to the apostles. They felt the wind blow, and small flames appeared over their heads. They were filled with wisdom and courage. The apostles wanted to tell everyone about Jesus. They had exciting news to share.

"I will go to lands far away and teach people about Jesus," Thomas said. He traveled to Persia and India. He preached and baptized many people. He healed the sick and performed miracles in Jesus' name. His faith and courage helped him become a great missionary.

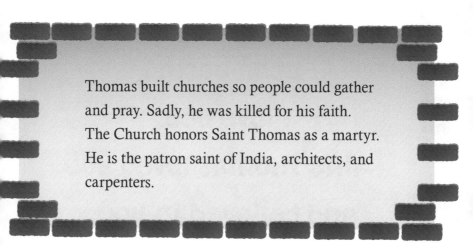

Thomas built churches so people could gather and pray. Sadly, he was killed for his faith. The Church honors Saint Thomas as a martyr. He is the patron saint of India, architects, and carpenters.

If you doubt what you cannot see,
Your faith will help you to believe.

Dear Jesus.

I love you.

Saint Thomas loved you
and believed in you.

He wanted to
know the truth.

Strengthen my faith
in you.

Help me to
build up your church.

Amen.

NEW WORDS (Glossary)

Apostle: One of the twelve special men chosen by Jesus to preach the Gospel

Architect: A person who plans and designs homes and buildings

Disciple: A person who follows the teachings of Jesus

Doubt: To question, or not believe in, something

Good News: The saving acts and words of God. Jesus died and rose again to give us forgiveness and eternal life.

Martyr: Someone who gives up his or her life on behalf of a belief or cause

Miracle: An amazing event that cannot be explained

Missionary: A person who teaches the faith or preaches the Gospel in a certain place

Persia: An ancient empire of the Middle East

Tomb: A place used for burying someone who has died

In the Gospel of John, Thomas is called "Didymus," a Greek name meaning "twin."

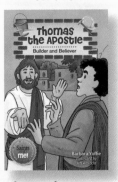